# Animal Shelters

**Written by James Talia**

Series Consultant: Linda Hoyt

WorldWise™
Content-based Learning

# Contents

Chapter 1

Chapter 2

Chapter 3

## Chapter 1

# A place to live

Many animals living in the wild have no need for a shelter, but for some animals a shelter helps them to survive.

Some animals need a shelter to raise their young and to protect themselves from the weather and from dangerous **predators**. Many use the same shelter throughout their lifetime. Some only use a shelter when they are giving birth or hatching eggs.

Some animals are expert builders and spend a long time making their homes. There are many kinds of ways that animals make their shelters. They can dig them or **weave** them or build them. Some even carry them around. Some animals find a shelter that another animal has left behind. Others find a place under a tree or among branches that they use as a shelter. When finding or making a place to shelter, animals always choose somewhere close to where they find food.

How many animal shelters can you find?

Places that animals use for shelter:

# Nests
# Burrows
# Dens
# Hollows
# Hives
# Colonies
# Shells

Can you think of any more?

# Chapter 2
# Builders

## Making a nest

Many animals use a nest for shelter. Animals also look after or hatch their **offspring** in a nest. Some animals build nests using mud or clay but they can also use grass, weeds, twigs and sticks to build a nest. Birds sometimes use material like plastic, rubbish or paper to build their nests.

## Ospreys

Ospreys build their nests from twigs, mosses, grasses and bark. They usually build the nest near the top of a tree. An osprey's nest can be about 1.5 metres wide and up to two metres deep. Ospreys build strong nests because they use the same nest for up to 20 years.

## Weaver ants

Weaver ants are found in the tropics. They make their nests from tree leaves. Worker ants hold the edges of leaves together, while other workers carry **larvae** that can spin silk back and forth across the edges. The larvae make sheets of silk that **bind** the leaves together.

## Weaver birds

Weaver birds **weave** their nests. Weaver birds' nests provide the best protection from **predators** like tree snakes, and also help attract a mate. The male weaver birds usually build their nests in trees that are covered with thorns. They tear long strips from palm fronds, grasses or weeds. They tie knots using their beak and feet, and then weave strips together to make the nest.

## Swans

Swans need to make their nests where foxes and other predators can't reach them. They build large floating nests in shallow water. Swans make their nests from reeds, water-weeds and grasses.

# Alligator research

My name is Rena and I am a **biologist**. This spring I am doing some research on alligators. I visit three alligator nests each day. I observe the nest, watch for any alligator activity, note if there are other animals around, and describe things that might help us understand more about these animals. I keep a record with a **code** for each nesting site and notes about anything important that I see.

### GN#34  June 21

Today I watched the large female alligator at this site building her nest. She gathered different kinds of plant materials including leaves and sticks, and made a large mound like a **compost** heap. The rotting plant material provides the heat that will incubate her eggs. She also dug up lots of mud and added that to her nest. Her nest is in a sheltered spot close to the water. The nesting mound is high enough to keep her eggs out of the water.

### GN#23  June 29

I was lucky enough to observe the young female at this site laying eggs today. She dug down 30 to 60 centimetres into her nesting mound to lay her eggs. When she had finished laying, she covered the eggs and lay on top of the mound to pack the plant material down on them. This does two things. It helps keep the eggs safe from predators and it keeps the nest warmer. She will return to lay more eggs over a two-week period.

### GN#41 July 8

Got up at dawn today while it was still cool. We visited nest 41 in our boat to measure the temperature in the nest. Alligators are not very active when the temperature is below 21°C, and they don't feed when the weather is cool. This was scary stuff and we didn't want to take any chances! My partner watched out for the female that guards the nest, while I checked the temperature. The temperature at the top of the nest was 29°C, and at the bottom it was 34°C.

### GN#23 July 30

Visited this site again today and saw a raccoon heading towards the nest. Raccoons love to eat alligator eggs, but this one was in for a surprise. Just as it got to the nest, the female came charging down the bank and into the water, hissing loudly and snapping her jaws. The raccoon got such a fright that it couldn't get out of there quickly enough. Female alligators stay close to their nests and guard them from predators like raccoons, coyotes, opossums, skunks and crows.

### GN#34 September 6

Today is the 65th day since the female at this site finished laying her eggs. As I approached the site I could hear a high-pitched chirping noise. The alligator was busy digging the nest open at the top and collecting some of the eggs in her mouth to take them to the water's edge. There she carefully cracked the eggs with her teeth and opened her mouth to release the hatchlings. She did this until all her young were freed from the nest.

# A hollow home

Some animals use a hollow for shelter. They find a small hole in a tree or a fallen branch. A few birds are specially designed to dig or peck their own tree hollow. Some mammals and reptiles also use a hollow for a shelter.

## Woodpeckers

Woodpeckers peck hollows into trees. They can do this because they have strong head and neck muscles, a very strong beak, and a thick skull. It takes many days and a lot of hard work for a woodpecker to complete its hollow.

**Thinking like a zoologist**

Birds are not the only animals to shelter in tree hollows. Can you think of other animals that use tree hollows for shelter?

## Hornbills

The hornbill also builds a shelter in a tree hollow. The female hornbill digs a hole in a tree trunk with her beak. When she has made the hollow, she closes it up and hatches her eggs inside. The male hornbill feeds her and the chicks through a very tiny opening – just big enough for his beak to fit through. When the chicks get bigger, the female breaks through the opening of the hollow so she can help the male to feed the chicks.

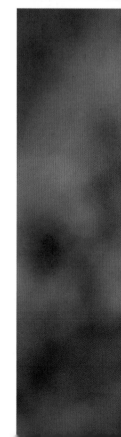

## Building tools for a woodpecker

- A very powerful chisel-shaped beak
- A thick **absorbent** skull
- Sharp claws
- Stiff tail feathers that help them perch on the side of a tree to make their hollow

## Living in a hole

Birds that find shelter in hollows include:

**Parrots**
**Owls**
**Kestrels**
**Flycatchers**
**Martins**
**Kingfishers**

## Red squirrels

Red squirrels spend most of their lives in trees. They build their nests in tree hollows or in the branches of a tree. Their nests are made from twigs, and are lined inside with moss, leaves, grass and bark. Red squirrels raise their young in these nest hollows and use the hollows for protection from the cold and from rain.

## Raccoons

Raccoons that live in wooded areas find shelter in the hollows of trees and logs. Raccoons use these shelters to protect themselves and their young from predators, and to rest while conserving energy during the winter months. Though they are sometimes active during the daytime, raccoons hunt and search for food at night. During the daytime or when the weather is cold, they spend much of their time asleep in their den.

## Bats

Most kinds of bats need a place to rest (roost) during the daytime. Many of these bats rest in tree hollows, where they are protected from the weather and from predators.

Monitor lizard

## Lizards

Monitor lizards make nesting hollows to lay their eggs. They make their hollows in different places. Some scratch a hollow in a tree, some **excavate** a hollow in the ground, and others dig into termite mounds. Termite mounds are kept warm by the termites, and these warm conditions help the monitors' eggs incubate. The termites also repair the damage to their mound and hide the monitor eggs from predators.

Termite mound

13

# A mud home

Some birds collect small lumps of mud or clay to make their nests.

### Swallows

Swallows build mud nests under a veranda or inside a roof. The nests are safe from predators, and the bird and the nest stay dry when it rains.

### Flamingos

Flamingos live near lakes or in shallow **lagoons**. They use mud to build a mound in the shape of a volcano. The nest is built above the water level so the flamingo's eggs are safe from predators.

### Magpie larks

Magpie larks make their nests in a high branch of a tree. They use mud to build a strong cup-shaped nest that they line with feathers and grass.

### Ovenbirds

The ovenbird of Central and South America builds a two-roomed clay nest. The nest has a narrow entrance that divides the nest into two rooms – an inner **chamber** and an outer chamber. The female lines the inner chamber with grass and feathers, and lays her eggs here. Heat gets trapped inside the inner chamber and helps the eggs to hatch.

**Find out more**

Why are magpie larks sometimes called mudlarks?

Chapter 3

# Digging in!

Prairie dogs dig underground tunnels in the desert. Platypuses dig a burrow inside the bank of a river or creek. Polar bears dig into the ice to make a shelter. Read the questions and answers to learn why and how these animals dig their shelters.

## **Distribution**
Prairie dogs are found in parts of central-western North America from southern Canada to northern Mexico.

## **Find out more**
Prairie dogs live in groups called colonies. The largest colony of prairie dogs was found in 1901, in Texas. How big was this colony? What size area did it cover?

## Prairie dogs

**Q. Where do prairie dogs shelter?**

**A.** Prairie dogs build large **networks** of tunnels called towns. Sometimes there are 50 or more tunnels linked to one main burrow. In each tunnel there are places for toilets, for eating and for sleeping.

**Q. How do prairie dogs dig their tunnels?**

**A.** Prairie dogs' hands and feet are called paws. They have sharp claws on their paws. They use these sharp claws and their short legs to dig underground tunnels on plains and grasslands. Prairie dog tunnels are built so the wind can flow through and keep the tunnel cool in summer.

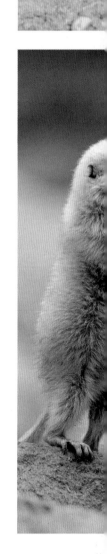

**Animals that prey on prairie dogs:**

**Badgers**
**Bobcats**
**Coyotes**
**Eagles**
**Falcons**
**Ferrets**
**Hawks**

Can you think of any more?

**Q. How many prairie dogs live in a town?**

A. Many hundreds of family groups live in the towns. A family group can have up to 15 prairie dogs. Each family group lives in their own tunnels inside the town.

**Q. Do prairie dogs ever leave their towns?**

A. Prairie dogs come out of their burrows only in the daytime to feed. They mostly eat plants, but sometimes they eat grasshoppers and other insects. While they are eating, a few prairie dogs watch for **predators**. These guards signal danger to one another by making loud barking or chirping noises. A single cry from one guard sends all the prairie dogs diving for safety. During the coldest part of the year prairie dogs remain **dormant** inside their tunnels.

# Platypuses

**Distribution**

Platypuses are found in eastern and southern parts of Australia.

**Q.  Where do platypuses shelter?**

A.  Platypuses dig their shelters, called burrows, inside the banks of creeks, rivers or swamps.  They dig a tunnel just above the water level.  The tunnel leads to a nesting burrow where the female platypus lays her eggs and looks after her young.  Platypuses build separate camping burrows for resting.

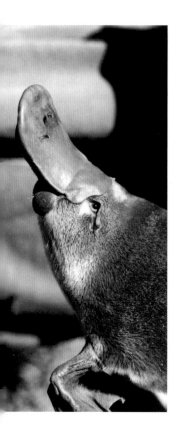

**Q. How do platypuses dig a burrow?**

A. The female platypus uses the claws on her front feet to dig a burrow. She pushes the soil behind her legs and packs it down with her flat tail. She takes about two weeks to dig her nesting burrow. Each burrow has a main tunnel and several dead-end smaller tunnels off the main one. The tunnels are between five and 15 metres long.

**Q. What do platypuses do in their burrow?**

A. When a female platypus is taking care of her young she stays in a nesting burrow. When a platypus is resting, it stays in a camping burrow. Platypuses build many camping burrows around the rivers and streams near where they feed.

**Q. Do platypuses ever leave their burrows?**

A. Platypuses spend up to 17 hours a day in their burrows. They leave their burrows to find food. Platypuses eat worms and insects that live in water. When they leave the burrow, they block the entrance so that predators can't get in.

**Animals that prey on platypuses:**

**Hawks**
**Eagles**
Owls
Crocodiles
**Water rats**
Foxes
Dogs
Cats

Can you think of any more?

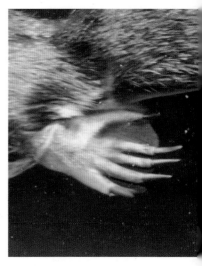

**Building tools:**
- Strong claws on the front feet to dig with
- A flat tail to pack the soil down when digging
- Webbed feet for swimming

# Polar bears

## Distribution

Polar bears are found in the area around the North Pole known as the Arctic Circle. This includes some of the coldest places on Earth such as parts of Alaska, Canada, Norway, Russia and Greenland.

**Q. Where do polar bears shelter?**

A. Polar bear shelters are called dens. The den is a short tunnel that has been dug into the ice.

**Q. How do polar bears make a den?**

A. In early winter a polar bear finds a place that is sheltered from the wind by huge pieces of ice. Snow builds up against the ice and makes a **snowdrift**. The polar bear uses its large powerful claws to dig a tunnel into the ice and make a den. The den is usually only about two metres long and big enough for one or two polar bears.

## Think about ...

1. The advantages of living in a den.

2. The disadvantages of living in a den.

3. The kind of body features needed to live underground.

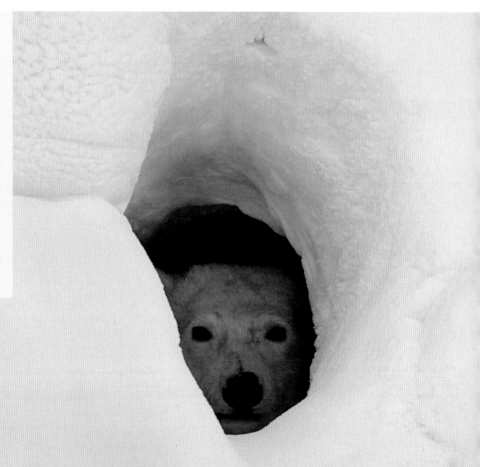

**Q. Do polar bears live in the den all year?**

A. Most polar bears spend only the coldest part of the year in a den. However, pregnant polar bears spend all winter inside a maternity den. The cubs are born without hair, but the warmth of the mother's breath heats up the den so that it is about 40°C inside and the cubs stay warm.

**Q. When do polar bears leave their dens?**

A. As soon as the coldest part of the year is over, polar bears leave the den and live outside on the ice. A mother and her cubs will stay in the den until the cubs are big enough to go onto the ice.

**Animals that prey on polar bears:**

**Humans Orca or killer whales**

Can you think of any more?

**Building tools:**
- Large paws
- Powerful claws on front feet
- Large powerful bodies

Chapter 4

# Building grand shelters

## Bees and termites

Some animals such as honeybees and termites live in large groups called colonies. Insects that live together in large groups are called social insects.

The chart below shows the similarities and differences between how honeybees and termites live.

| | Honeybees |
|---|---|
| **What is the shelter called?** | Beehive |
| **Where are the shelters made?** | Tree branches, walls, tree hollows, small rock openings |
| **What lives in the shelter?** | Queen, worker bees, drones |
| **What happens inside?** | The queen lays the eggs.<br>The workers build the hive, put the eggs in the cells, look after the young, collect **pollen**, make honey and clean the hive.<br>The drones mate with new queen bees. |
| **What is the shelter made from?** | Bees build a shelter with wax. They make wax in a small gland under their abdomen. The wax is a **lightweight** but sturdy building material. |
| **How is the shelter made?** | Bees mix the wax with saliva, sap or resin from plants. They use the mixture to build six-sided cells that make the hive. |

## Termites

Termite mound

Underground, above ground

Queen, king, soldiers, workers, reproductive swarmers

The queen lays the eggs.
The king mates with the queen and continues to fertilise the eggs.
The soldiers guard the mound.
The workers build the mound, gather food, care for the eggs and look after the young.  The reproductive swarmers leave the mound to mate and start new colonies.

Termites build a shelter with soil.  They mix the soil with saliva.

The mixture of earth and saliva makes a type of cement. This mixture is used to build the mound.

**Honeybees and termites need to control the temperature inside their hive or mound.**

- Honeybees fan their wings to keep the air around them cool.
- Termites make tiny holes in the top of their mound so that the heat can escape.

# Building a beaver lodge

Beavers live together in family groups in a shelter called a **lodge**. Their lodge is made in the middle of a dam or pond, which the beavers build from stones, tree logs and mud. The dam or pond protects beavers from **predators**, and it is also where they find their food. The beavers live inside the lodge where it is warm and dry.

Beavers are known for their great skill at cutting down trees with their strong front teeth. They eat the bark and use the branches to build their shelters.

**Find out more**

Beavers are excellent swimmers and divers. A beaver can swim underwater for just over one kilometre. How do beavers swim so far? How many beavers might live in a beaver lodge? Who makes up a family of beavers?

**Making a lodge**

**1** Beavers cut down trees with their strong front teeth. They eat the bark from the trees.

**2** Beavers use wood, stones and mud to make a dam. The dam holds back the water and forms large ponds.

**Building tools:**
- Large, strong front teeth that work like chisels for cutting down trees
- Front feet like fingers that can hold branches and sticks
- Webbed back feet for swimming

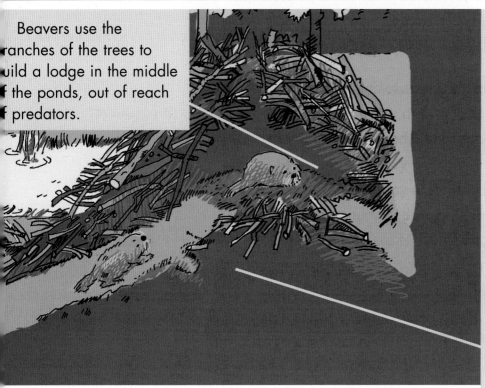

Beavers use the branches of the trees to build a lodge in the middle of the ponds, out of reach of predators.

**4** A lodge has underwater entrances and tunnels that lead to an inside **chamber**. The floor of the chamber is always above the height of the water. Beavers are born in the chamber, where they stay warm and dry in winter.

# Chapter 5

# Shelters on the move

## Use your mum

### Shelter in her pouch

Marsupials are mammals that have a special way of looking after their young. The young are born tiny and helpless, and they make their way into a part of their mother's body called the pouch.

The pouch is a warm safe place, and the young feed on their mother's milk from inside the pouch. Young kangaroos do this. They live in their mother's pouch until they are about nine months old. They travel everywhere in this pouch until they are ready to feed themselves.

## Shelter on her back

The female wolf spider carries her egg sac on her body. When the tiny spiderlings hatch, they climb onto their mother's back. The spiderlings cling to the hairs on their mother's back, and she carries them around as she hunts and feeds. The spiderlings leave her when they can feed themselves.

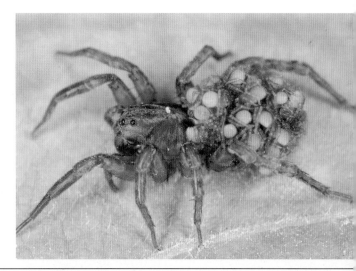

## Shelter on her stomach

Sea otters are born in the ocean. When they are born, sea otter pups can't swim. They have their eyes open, and their thick coats of hair help them to float, but they don't start to swim until they are about two months old. The mother carries her pup on her stomach until it can swim and dive on its own.

# Grow your own

Some animals take their homes with them wherever they go! Tortoises, snails and shellfish all have a hard shell that is attached to their bodies. This hard shell acts as a shelter from the weather, and it helps protect the animal against **predators**.

### The giant tortoise

The giant tortoise has a shell made from tough layers of horn and bone. As the tortoise grows, its shell grows too. When the tortoise senses danger, it pulls its head inside the shell for protection.

### Snails

Snails don't like hot, dry weather. When the weather becomes too dry or hot, snails go into their shells and seal the entrance. They also hide inside their shells when they are disturbed. Snails can't survive without shells.

### Nautilus

The nautilus lives in deep water, and its body is protected from predators by a shell. The nautilus adds new chambers to its shell as it grows. These chambers are filled with gas and water. The nautilus adjusts the levels of water and gas to allow it to float and become more bouyant. It moves by pushing water through its body.

## Scallops

Scallops have a fan-shaped shell that they can open and close to help them swim through water. The shell protects the scallop's soft body from harm. Their shell grows as they get bigger.

**Did you know?**
The largest land snail ever to be recorded was a giant African snail found in Sierra Leone. It weighed about nine kilograms and its shell was neary 40 centimetres long.

29

# Find one that fits

### Hermit crabs

Hermit crabs have soft bodies that can be easily damaged. They protect themselves by taking shelter in a dead animal's shell. When a mollusc dies and leaves an empty shell, a hermit crab can use it for shelter. The hermit crab grips the inside of the mollusc shell with its back legs and carries this new home around. When it grows too big for the shell, it simply finds another one that fits!

### Golden-shouldered and hooded parrots

Some animals use the shelter of another animal to lay their eggs. Golden-shouldered and hooded parrots make a hollow in a termite mound. When it rains, the earth in the termite mound is soft, and the parrots make a hollow in which they lay and **incubate** their eggs.

## Design your own animal

Design a new animal.

Think about:

1. What kind of food will the animal eat?
2. What kinds of animals eat the new animal?
3. What kind of habitat will the animal live in?
4. What kind of shelter will the animal need?
5. What kind of body features will the animal have?

Draw a picture of the animal and write labels.

# Glossary

**absorbent** something that can take an impact

**bind** to make something stay together

**biologist** a person who studies living things

**chamber** a private place where something might sleep

**code** a system of symbols that have a meaning

**compost** a pile of rotting plant matter

**dormant** asleep

**excavate** to dig out an area and make it hollow

**incubate** keeping eggs at the right temperature so they will hatch

**lagoon** a shallow body of water

**larvae** the newly hatched wormlike form of many insects

**lightweight** something that is not heavy and often flimsy

**lodge** a shelter made from wood

**network** a series of passages linked together

**offspring** the animal that is born or hatched from a parent

**pollen** a fine powdery material produced by flowering plants

**predators** animals that kill and eat other animals

**snowdrift** a bank of snow formed by the wind

**weave** to make something by winding strips of material over and under one another

# Index